T0083159

The Miracle of the Spring

Bob Chilcott

for SATB and percussion

Vocal score

MUSIC DEPARTMENT

OXFORD
UNIVERSITY PRESS

OXFORD
UNIVERSITY PRESS

Great Clarendon Street, Oxford OX2 6DP,
United Kingdom

Oxford University Press is a department of the University of Oxford.
It furthers the University's objective of excellence in research, scholarship,
and education by publishing worldwide. Oxford is a registered trade mark of
Oxford University Press in the UK and in certain other countries

© Oxford University Press 2015

Bob Chilcott has asserted his right under the Copyright, Designs
and Patents Act, 1988, to be identified as the Composer of this Work

Database right Oxford University Press (maker)

First published 2015

Impression: 1

All rights reserved. No part of this publication may be reproduced,
stored in a retrieval system, or transmitted, in any form or by any means,
without the prior permission in writing of Oxford University Press

Permission to perform this work in public (except in the course of divine worship)
should normally be obtained from the Performing Right Society Ltd (PRS) at
www.prsformusic.com or a local performing right licensing organization, unless
the owner or the occupier of the premises being used already holds a licence from
such an organization. Likewise, permission to make and exploit a recording must
be obtained in advance from the Mechanical-Copyright Protection Society Ltd
(MCPS) at www.prsformusic.com or a local mechanical copyright licensing
organization

Enquiries concerning reproduction outside the scope of the above
should be directed to the Music Rights Department, Oxford University Press,
at music.permissions.uk@oup.com or at the address above

ISBN 978-0-19-340062-7

Music and text origination by Andrew Jones
Printed in Great Britain on acid-free paper by
Halstan & Co. Ltd, Amersham, Bucks.

Contents

1. Where water waits 4

2. The source of the spring 12

3. To sing of water 19

4. The desert 22

5. The voice of water 26

Composer's note

The Miracle of the Spring was written for Magdalen College School, Oxford, in 2014. The Director of Music, John Cullen, wanted a piece for choir and percussion instruments in the vein of my earlier work *The Making of the Drum*. I had read a poem by Charles Bennett, which I loved, on the subject of water, and I asked him to expand the idea into a suite of five poems, which ultimately make up the texts for this piece. The idea also reflected a conversation I'd had on a visit to the United States about the importance of water to all of us. In the cycle, I have used the glockenspiel and bell tree to depict the flow and sparkle of water, and a pair of log drums to reflect the dryness of the desert. The discovery of the spring at the end of the piece reminds us of the life-giving properties of water and how much we need to respect and value it as one of our greatest resources.

The percussion parts may be performed by members of the choir or separate percussionists.

Duration: *c.*12 minutes

for Jon Cullen and the Choir of Magdalen College School, Oxford

The Miracle of the Spring

Charles Bennett (b. 1954)

BOB CHILCOTT

1. Where water waits

* Percussion 1: glockenspiel (or similar, e.g. metallophone) and log drums. Percussion 2: bell tree/mark tree and log drums. The part for log drums (movements 3 and 4) should be performed by both percussionists, using drums of different sizes/pitches. Separate percussion parts are available to download from www.oup.com.

Music © Oxford University Press 2015. Text © Charles Bennett. Reproduced by permission of the author.

Printed in Great Britain

OXFORD UNIVERSITY PRESS, MUSIC DEPARTMENT, GREAT CLARENDON STREET, OXFORD OX2 6DP

The Moral Rights of the Composer have been asserted. Photocopying this copyright material is ILLEGAL.

10
gliss.
gliss.
mp
blue sky, per - haps I'll find the place, the place where
mp
wa - ter waits, where wa - ter, where wa - ter waits, per - haps I'll find the place, the place where
mp
a blue sky, where wa - ter, where wa - ter waits,
mp
a blue sky, find the place where
mp

15
gliss.
gliss.
p
wa - ter waits. Or may - be the
p
wa - ter, where wa - ter waits, where wa - ter, where wa - ter waits, where wa - ter, where
wa - ter, wa - - ter waits.
wa - ter, wa - - ter waits.
p

20
gliss.
gliss.
cresc.
cac - tus wren, who drinks from white blos - som,
cresc.
wa - ter waits, where wa - ter, where wa - ter waits, where wa - ter, where wa - ter waits, where
p
cresc.
The cac - tus wren, white
p
cresc.
The cac - tus wren, white
cresc.
25
gliss.
gliss.
mf
dim.
will show me where the flower of wa - ter o - pens,
mf
dim.
wa - ter, where wa - ter waits, will show me where the flower of wa - ter, wa - ter, where
mf
dim.
blos - - som, where wa - ter, where wa - ter waits, where wa - ter waits,
mf
dim.
blos - - som, show me wa - ter, wa - ter
mf
dim.

30
mp
p
will show me where the flower of wa - ter o - pens.
wa - ter waits, where wa - ter, where wa - ter waits, where wa - ter, where wa - ter waits, where
show where wa - ter o - pens.
o - pens, show where wa - ter o - pens.
35
gliss.
mp cresc.
If I sip the burn - ing air as if it were a
wa - ter, where wa - ter waits. Sip, I sip the burn - ing air as if it were a
Sip the burn - ing air as if a
Sip the air as if a

40
mf cresc.
ques - tion, per - haps I'll learn to taste, per-haps I'll learn to taste, to taste the smell of
ques - tion, per - haps I'll learn to taste, per-haps I'll learn to taste, to taste the smell of
ques - tion, per - haps I'll learn to taste, per-haps I'll learn to taste, to taste the smell of
ques - tion, per - haps I'll learn to taste, learn to taste the smell of
45
f
mf
gliss.
mf dim.
wa - ter,
div.
unis.
wa - ter, wa - ter, wa - ter, of wa - -
wa - ter, wa - ter, wa - ter, where wa - ter, where
wa - ter, where wa - ter waits, where wa - ter, where wa - ter waits, wa - -
wa - ter, wa - ter, wa - ter, wa - ter,
wa - ter, of wa - - ter, of wa - -

50
gliss.
-ter.
At
wa - ter waits, where wa - ter, where wa - ter waits, where wa - ter, where wa - ter waits, where
-ter.
-ter.
55
gliss.
gliss.
night the bril - liant stars are rain - drops in
wa - ter, where wa - ter waits, where wa - ter, where wa - ter waits, where wa - ter, where
The bril - liant stars,
The bril - liant stars,

60
gliss.
gliss.
mf
hea - ven, each of them rea - dy to
mf
wa - ter waits, where wa - ter, where wa - ter waits, each of them rea - dy, where
mf
in hea - - ven, where wa - ter, where wa - ter waits to
mf
in hea - - ven, each rea - dy to
mf
65
gliss.
gliss.
mp
fall, to fall, as the light of wa - ter,
mp
wa - ter, where wa - ter waits, where wa - ter, where wa - ter waits, where wa - ter, where
fall, fall,
fall, fall,
mp

70
gliss.
gliss.
gliss.
p
as the light of wa - ter, as the light of wa - ter.
p
wa - ter waits, where wa - ter, where wa - ter waits, where wa - ter, where wa - ter waits, where
mp
p
wa - - - ter, wa - - - ter, wa - -
mp
p
wa - - - ter, wa - - - ter, wa - -
p
75
rit.
to Log Drums (mov. 3)
to Log Drums (mov. 3)
rit.
wa - ter, where wa - ter waits, where wa - ter, where wa - ter, wa - ter waits.
- ter.
- ter.
rit.

2. *The source of the spring*

* Change from 'waits' to 'oo' at the beginning of the bar, maintaining a continuous sound.

9
strand-ed there.
To - day I'll re-pair its hull
and heal the gash where its
oo
oo
oo
12
A. OLO
float-ing was bro-ken by a stone.
S.
p legato
To - night I'll make an oar from a
A.
p legato
To - night I'll make an oar from a
T.
p legato
To - night from a
B.
p legato
To - night a
p legato

* Small notes = alternative line

21
source of the spring.
source of the spring.
source of the spring.
source of the spring.
p
oo
25
S. SOLO
A. SOLO
In the bed of a dried-up ri - ver I found a bro-ken
In the bed of a dried-up ri - ver I found a bro-ken boat,
S.
A.
T.
B.

28
boat,
To - day I'll re-pair its hull
swept a - way by floods and strand ed there.
To - day I'll re-pair its hull and
p
mm
oo
oo
oo
oo
oo
31
and heal the gash.
heal the gash where its float - ing was bro - ken by a stone.
p dolcis.
mm
To -
p dolcis.
oo
To -
p dolcis.
oo
To -
p dolcis.
oo
To -
p dolcis.

34
p dolcis.
S. SOLO
To - night from a de - sert tree and row my - self to
S.
-night I'll make an oar from a de - sert tree and row my - self to sleep by
A.
-night I'll make an oar from a de - sert tree and row my - self to sleep by
T.
- night from a de - sert tree, row by
B.
-night a de - sert tree, row a
37
mp
sleep. To - mor - row I'll go where I'm ta - ken,
fol - low - ing a star. To - mor - row I'll drift on a lake and go where I am ta - ken, un -
fol - low - ing a star. To - mor - row I'll drift on a lake and go where I am ta - ken, un -
fol - low - ing a star. To - mor - row I'm ta - - ken,
star. To - mor - row I'm ta - - ken,

40
I find the source of the spring.
- til in the end I find the source of the spring.
- til in the end I find the source of the spring.
in the end the source of the spring.
in the end the source of the spring.
p
oo
43
rit.
pp
S.
A.
T.
B.

3. To sing of water

20
cresc.
f
wa - - - - ter, wa - - - - ter, wa - ter.
cresc.
wa - ter.
fish made out of stone but still swim - ming,
wa - ter. Sing
f
cresc.
wa - ter.
24
f
Go down, go down deep e - nough and you'll find the place, you'll
of wa - ter, wa - ter, to sing of wa - ter,
f Sing of wa - ter, wa - ter, to sing of wa - ter,
28
find the place where a wave is wait - ing to break. To
wa - ter, sing, to sing of wa - ter,
sing of wa - ter, sing, to sing of wa - ter,
32
wa - ter, wa -
mp
sing of wa - ter, wa - ter, to sing of wa - ter, wa - ter.
sing of wa - ter, to sing of wa - ter.
sing of wa - ter, sing of wa - ter, wa - ter.

37
Log Drums (two players)
mp
- - - - - - - ter, wa - - - - - - ter,
Un - der our feet is a sea. I feel it call in my blood as
42
cresc.
f
wa - - - ter, wa - - - ter, wa - ter.
if I were a fish who longed for the o - cean, o - cean.
To sing of wa - ter,
To sing of
47
ff
wa - ter, to sing of wa - ter, wa - ter, to sing of wa - ter, wa - ter, to
wa - ter, to sing of wa - ter, to sing of wa - ter, to
wa - ter, sing of wa - ter, to sing of wa - ter,
52
wa - ter,
sing of wa - ter, wa - ter, wa - ter,
sing of wa - ter, wa - ter,
wa - ter.
sing of wa - ter,

4. The desert

With driving rhythm ♩ = c.108
Log Drums (two players)
PERC. 1 & 2
ff
mf
S.
A.
T.
B.
(ff)
To the de - sert, to the de - sert,
7
I went to the de - sert be - cause I was so
to the de - sert, to the de - sert, to the de - sert, to the de - sert, to the de - sert,
to the de - sert, to the de - sert, to the de - sert, to the de - sert, to the de - sert,
12
dry, I knew the sand, the sand and rock would be like my
to the de - sert, to the de - sert, to the de - sert, to the de - sert, to the de - sert,
to the de - sert, to the de - sert, to the de - sert, to the de - sert, to the de - sert,
I knew the sand, the sand and rock would be like my

17
skin, like my skin.
to the de - sert, to the de - sert, to the de - sert, to the de - sert, de - sert.
to the de - sert, to the de - sert, to the de - sert, to the de - sert, de - sert.
skin, like my skin.
22
mf
To the de - sert, to the de - sert, to the de - sert, to the de - sert, to the de - sert,
I came to the de-
27
to the de - sert, to the de - sert, to the de - sert, to the de - sert, to the de - sert,
- sert be - cause I want - ed to taste
wa - ter that
32
to the de - sert, to the de - sert, to the de - sert, to the de - sert, to the de - sert,
fell as rain where the light was young, was young.

37
to the de - sert, de - sert.
In the de - sert, in the de - sert, in the de - sert,
42
S.
A.
in the de - sert, in the de - sert, in the de - sert, in the de - sert, in the de - sert,
T.
in the de - sert, in the de - sert, in the de - sert, in the de - sert, in the de - sert,
B.
I stayed in the de - sert be - cause I learned its name
47
in the de - sert, was a drop which washed me, in the de - sert, in the de - sert,
in the de - sert, was a drop which washed me, in the de - sert, in the de - sert,
was a drop which washed me clear of all my days, my

52
Perc. 1 to Glockenspiel
Perc. 2 to Bell Tree
fff
ff
in the de - sert, in the de - sert, in the de - sert, de - sert.
ff
in the de - sert, in the de - sert, in the de - sert, de - sert.
div.
ff
days, my days, de - sert.

Slower ♩ = c.60
56
I be - came the de - sert be - cause I want-ed you to come and
mp
mp and
mp
mm mm mm

rit.
64
p
let me show you what it means to drink, to drink, drink.
p
mm drink.

5. The voice of water

14
fade to nothing
fade to nothing
wa - ter, wa - ter.
fade to nothing
wa - ter, wa - ter.
fade to nothing
lan - guage be - neath these scorch-ing stones.
fade to nothing
20
p
The soft voice of wa - ter, soft voice of wa - ter ask - ing if I am
p
The soft voice of wa - ter, soft voice of wa - ter ask - ing if I am
p
Soft voice of wa - - - ter ask - ing if I am
p
Soft voice of wa - ter, wa - ter,
p

27
freely
p
gliss.
gliss.
gliss.
p
thirst - y, wa - ter, wa - ter, wa - ter,
thirst - y, wa - ter, wa - ter, wa - ter,
mp
thirst - y. How can it know I am
wa - - ter, wa - - - -
32
fade to nothing
fade to nothing
mp
wa - ter, wa - ter, wa - ter. O
fade to nothing
mp
wa - ter, wa - ter, wa - ter. O
mp
dry as an au - tumn leaf? O
mp
- - ter, wa - - - ter. O
fade to nothing
mp

38
freely
f
freely
gliss.
gliss.
f
f
wa - ter, rush to touch me, gush and dash in
f
wa - ter, rush to touch me, gush and dash in
f (quick and bright)
wa - ter, rush to wa - ter, gush and dash in
f
wa - ter, rush to touch me, gush and dash, dash
f
44
gliss.
gliss.
dim.
streams. O let me hear the tears a moun - tain
dim.
streams. O let me hear the tears, the tears,
dim.
wa - ter, let me hear the tears, the tears,
dim.
in streams. O let me hear the tears a moun - tain
dim.

50
mp
gliss.
gliss.
mp
cries.
p
O speak to me
mp
wa - ter.
fade to nothing
p
O speak to me
mp
wa - ter.
fade to nothing
p
O speak to me,
mp
cries.
p
Speak to
mp
p
56
now, speak to me now and I'll lis - ten by drink -
cresc.
now, speak to me now and I'll lis - ten by drink -
cresc.
O speak to me and I'll lis - ten by drink -
cresc.
me, to me, lis - ten by drink -
cresc.
cresc.

62
f
-ing. O let the voice of wa - ter sing in my
f
unis.
-ing. O let the voice of wa - ter sing in my
f
-ing. O let the voice of wa - ter sing in my
f
-ing. O let the voice of wa - ter sing in my
f
67
c.15 seconds
ff
dim.
mf
gliss.
gliss.
dim.
mf
ff
c.15 seconds
ff
dim.
mf
mouth, wa - ter,
ff
dim.
mf
mouth, wa - ter,
ff
dim.
mf
mouth, wa - ter,
ff
dim.
mf
mouth, wa - ter,
c.15 seconds
ff
ff
dim.
mf

70
freely
mf
mp
gliss.
wa - ter,
78
in tempo
p
rit.
pp
fade to nothing